DATE DUE		

BERRYESSA UNION
SCHOOL DISTRICT

TOYON SCHOOL LIBRARY
SAN JOSE, CALIF.

© 1992 Franklin Watts

Franklin Watts, Inc.
95 Madison Avenue
New York, NY 10016

Library of Congress Cataloging-in-Publication Data

Richardson, Joy.
    Heat / by Joy Richardson.
      p. cm. — (Picture science)
    Includes index.
    Summary: Briefly describes how heat is produced, conducted, used, and measured.
    ISBN 0-531-14239-6
    1. Heat — Juvenile literature. [1. Heat.] I. Title.
II. Series: Richardson, Joy. Picture science.
QC256.R53 1993
536—dc20   92-14419
                     CIP AC

Editor: Sarah Ridley
Designer: Janet Watson
Illustrator: Linda Costello

Photographs: Bubbles Photo Library title page, 16, 28; Collections/Anthea Sieveking 25; Chris Fairclough Colour Library cover, 7, 19, 20; Chris Fairclough/F Watts 23; Sally and Richard Greenhill 13, 26; Robert Harding Picture Library 8, 14; ZEFA 11.

Printed in Singapore

All rights reserved

PICTURE SCIENCE

HEAT

Joy Richardson

FRANKLIN WATTS
New York • London • Toronto • Sydney

Heat rays

When a fire burns it sends out heat.
You cannot see the heat but
you can feel it touching you.

Rays of heat spread out in
straight lines from the fire.

If you stretch out your hands
they catch the heat.
If you put them behind your back
the heat rays cannot reach them.

Heat from the sun

The sun sends out heat which travels through space.

On a hot sunny day you can feel heat, straight from the sun, touching your skin.

If a cloud moves across the sun or you move into the shade, you can feel the heat rays being blocked off.

Hot air

The sun's rays heat the earth.
The warm earth heats up the air.
That is why the air stays warm
even when the sun goes in.

Hot air is lighter than cold air,
so warm air rises up into the sky.

When the warm air cools
it sinks down again.
Air is always on the move.
This makes breezes and winds.

warm air rises

cool air sinks

Heating rooms

Rooms can be heated
by warming up the air.

Fan heaters draw in cool air,
heat it up and blow it out.
The warm air rises and
circles around the room.

Radiators heat the air near them.
The warm air circles around and
soon the whole room warms up.

Hot metal

Metal is a good conductor of heat. Heat passes through it easily.

That is why radiators and saucepans are made of metal.

Heat passes through the metal saucepan and heats up the food inside.

A wooden spoon is good for stirring hot food in a saucepan. The handle stays cool because wood is a poor conductor of heat.

Keeping warm

Air is a very poor conductor of heat.
Heat does not pass through it easily.
So, air can help to keep you warm.

A woolen sweater traps a lot
of air between its fibers.
This means that heat from your
body cannot escape easily.

Fur and feathers trap the air
and keep animals warm.
Clothes keep you warm.

Materials that stop heat
escaping are good insulators.

Losing heat

Heat can soon be lost through windows, walls, and roofs.

Insulating material in the roof and inside hollow walls can help to keep the heat in. Insulation works like a blanket to keep the house warm.

Heat passes easily through glass. Double-glazed windows have a gap between two layers of glass. Heat has difficulty crossing the gap.

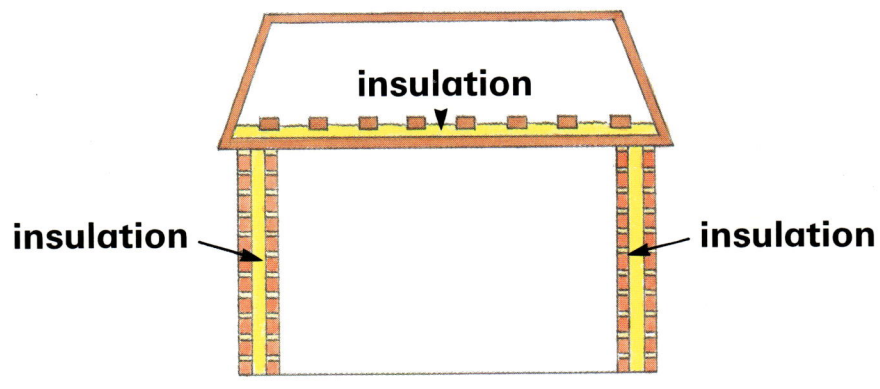

Hot food

Heat changes the food we eat.

Chocolate, butter, and jelly melt when they are heated.

Fruit and vegetables turn soft when they are cooked.

Bread becomes crusty when it is baked. Runny cake mixture rises and dries out in the oven.

Heat change

Heat can make solid things liquid.
Even glass and metal will melt
if they are heated very strongly.

Heat can turn liquid into a
gas which floats in the air.

When wet hair, damp towels,
and muddy ground dry out,
the water evaporates.
It changes into water vapor
and mixes with the air.

When water boils you can see
the water vapor rising
into the air as steam.

Measuring heat

Heat makes things expand and take up more space.

A thermometer measures temperature by showing how much expansion has taken place.

The liquid in a thermometer expands as it gets hotter.
It pushes up the tube to a higher mark.

When the temperature cools down the liquid shrinks again and shows a lower temperature.

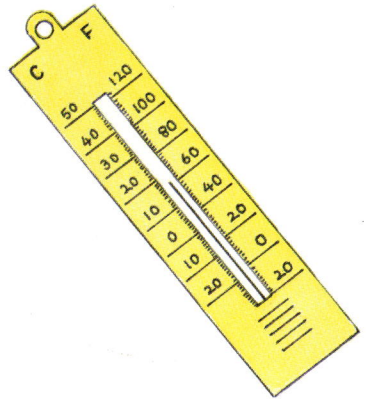

Hot and cold

If you put a thermometer
where it catches the sun,
the temperature may shoot up,
even though the air around is cool.

People skiing can get a suntan
without the snow melting.

Skin and clothes soak up the sun's rays.
Shining white snow reflects the rays.
They can bounce off without heating
the ground and warming up the air.

Heat inside you

Your body's temperature is meant to stay around 98·6° Fahrenheit.

Nerves carry messages from your skin to your brain about feeling hot or cold. Sweating and shivering help to keep you the right temperature.

We can adjust the heating or the clothes we wear to keep ourselves feeling comfortable.

Index

Air 10, 12, 17, 22, 27

Brain 28
Breeze 10

Clothes 17, 27, 28
Cloud 9
Conductor of heat 15, 17

Earth 10

Fan heaters 12
Feathers 17
Fire 6
Food 15, 21
Fur 17

Glass 18, 22

Heat 6, 9, 10, 12, 15, 17, 18, 21, 22, 24
Heat rays 6, 9

Insulation 18

Insulators 17

Liquid 22, 24

Metal 15, 22

Nerves 28

Radiators 12, 15

Saucepans 15
Skin 9, 27, 28
Space 9, 24
Steam 27
Sun 9, 10, 27

Temperature 24, 27, 28
Thermometer 24, 27

Water vapor 22
Wind 10
Wood 15

29